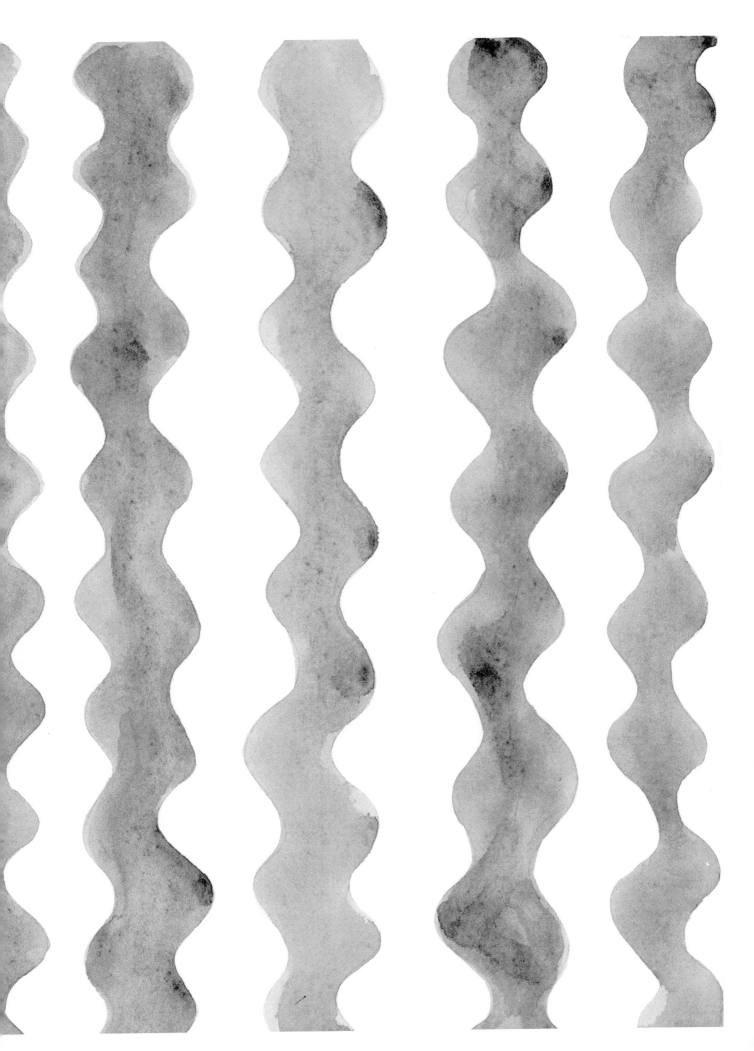

Dedicated to my husband and life partner, Mike,
and the two daughters we share,
Malika and Kendra.  You sweeten my life.

Order this book online at www.trafford.com
or email orders@trafford.com

Most Trafford titles are also available at major online book retailers.

**Trafford** www.trafford.com
**North America & international**
toll-free: 1 888 232 4444 (USA & Canada)
fax: 812 355 4082

Our mission is to efficiently provide the world's finest, most comprehensive book publishing
service, enabling every author to experience success. To find out how to publish your
book, your way, and have it available worldwide, visit us online at www.trafford.com

ISBN: 978-1-4251-5961-0 (sc)

Print information available on the last page.

Trafford rev. 03/16/2020

# Coffee with Cream

**H**ello, my name is Malika.  I am five years old.  My Momma says I am the color of coffee and cream with two spoons of sugar.  She says that is why I am so sweet.

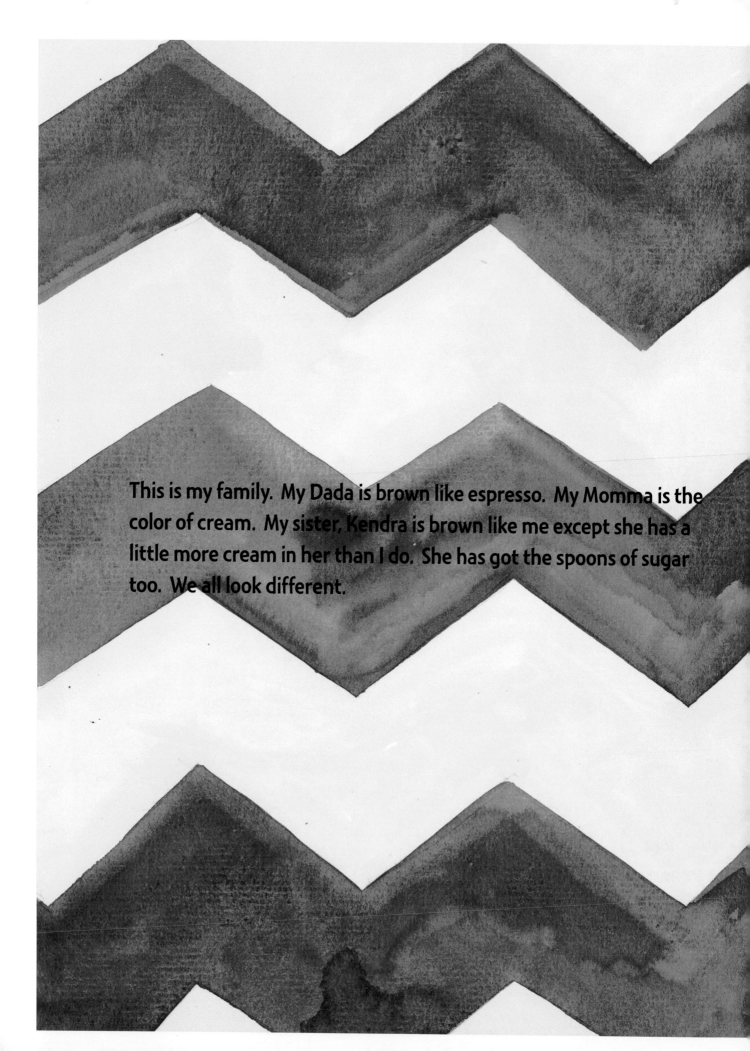

This is my family.  My Dada is brown like espresso.  My Momma is the color of cream.  My sister, Kendra is brown like me except she has a little more cream in her than I do.  She has got the spoons of sugar too.  We all look different.

I think my Momma is beautiful.

One day when I was four I asked Momma, "am I going to have cream colored skin like you when I grow up?"

She said "no."

I cried, "but I want to match you!"

"Oh sweetheart," she sighed, "we match in so many ways!  I'll get some paper and a pencil and we can make a list."

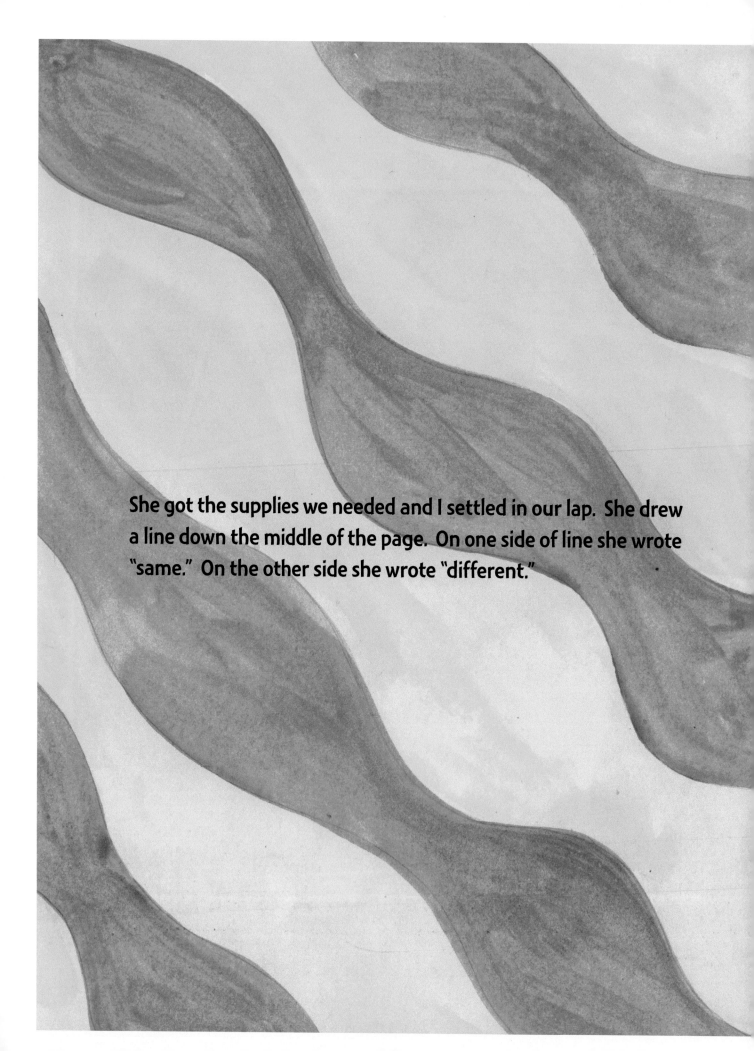

She got the supplies we needed and I settled in our lap. She drew a line down the middle of the page. On one side of line she wrote "same." On the other side she wrote "different."

"So, how are we the same?" she asked.

"We are both girls!" I answered.

"What else"

"We both have curly hair!  Brown eyes too!" I shouted.
Momma wrote on the paper.

"What else?" she asked.

"We are both artists!

"That is right!" she replied as she added "Artists" to the list.

"We both love to cook!" I said.

"And sing and dance!"

"We both love to cuddle and drink warm chocolate on a cold day!"
I said.

"We both love raw cookie dough," Momma added, "more than the
cookies when they are baked!" We laughed.
"We both love our family and friends," I said as I gave Momma a hug.

The "same" list was long.

| same | different |
|------|-----------|
| girls | |
| curly hair | |
| brown eyes | |
| Artists | |
| cook | |
| sing | |
| dance | |
| read | |
| talk | |
| listen | |
| cuddle | |
| warm cocoa | |
| raw dough | |
| family | |
| friends | |

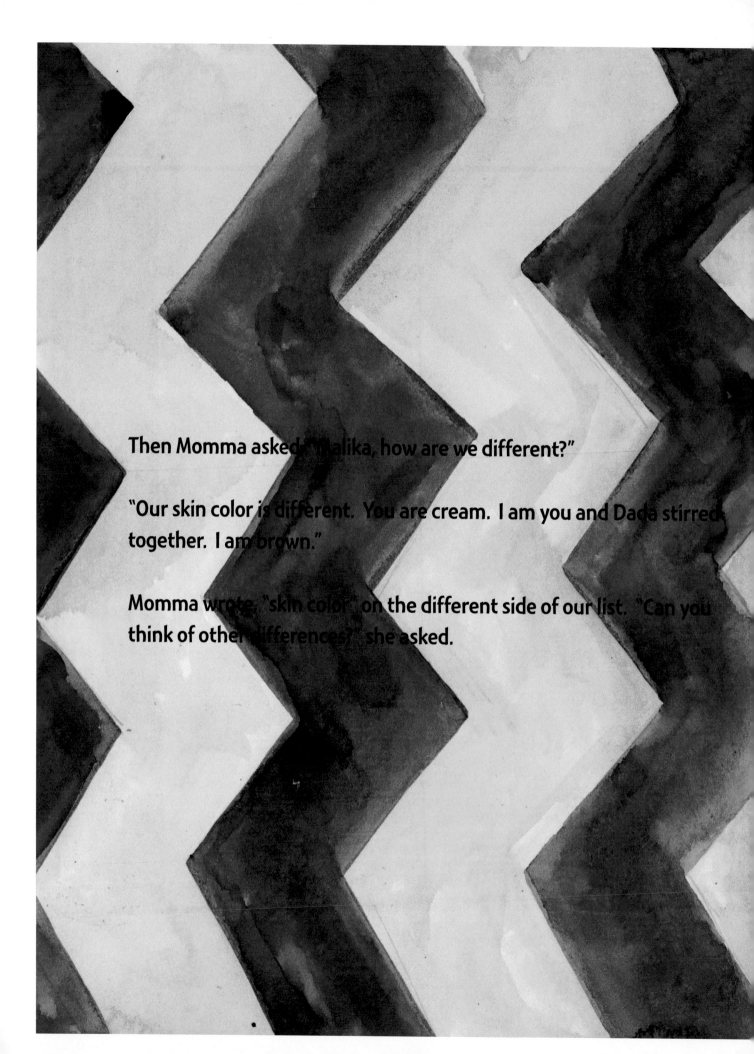

Then Momma asked, "Malika, how are we different?"

"Our skin color is different. You are cream. I am you and Dada stirred together. I am brown."

Momma wrote, "skin color" on the different side of our list. "Can you think of other differences?" she asked.

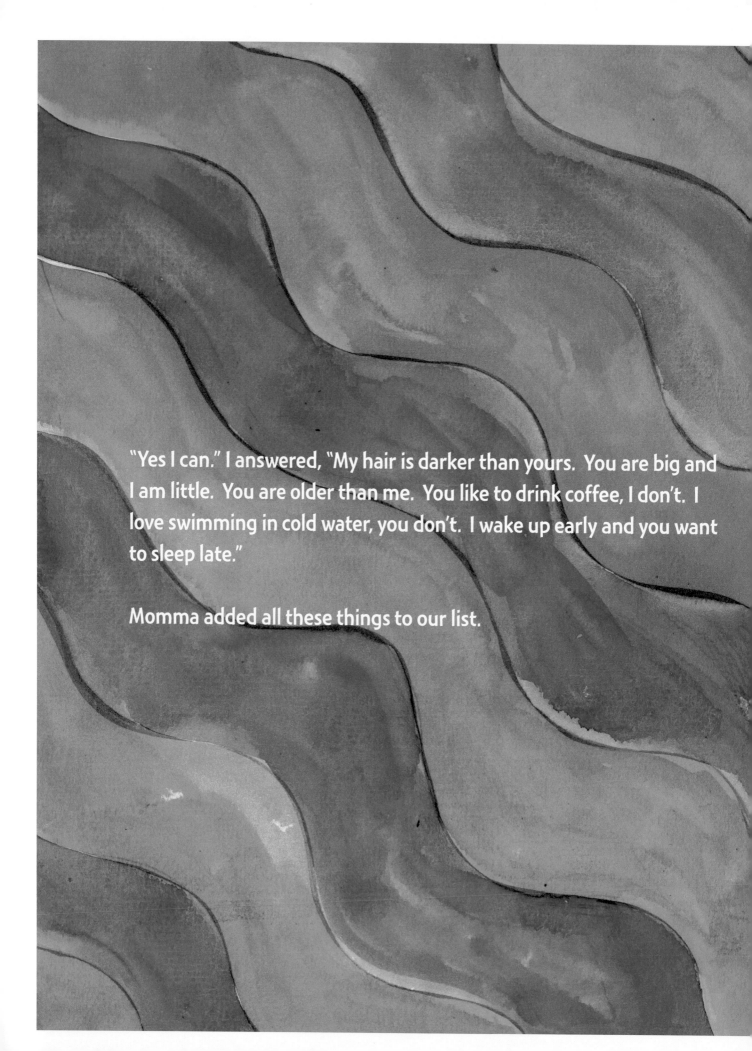

"Yes I can." I answered, "My hair is darker than yours. You are big and I am little. You are older than me. You like to drink coffee, I don't. I love swimming in cold water, you don't. I wake up early and you want to sleep late."

Momma added all these things to our list.

We looked at our list. "We are the same in so many important ways," she said as she held me. "These are the ways we will match when you grow up."

I smiled and gave my Momma a kiss on her nose. Then I said, "I love you!"

She grinned and said, "I love you too! That is another way we are alike."

| same | different |
|------|-----------|
|      |           |

Printed in the United States
By Bookmasters